## 「ビジネス英語」はむずかしい?

職場では、伝えたいことははっきりと、なおかつ丁寧な言葉を選ばなければいけないですよね。それが英語(外国語)となると、さらに気を使います。

「こういう言い方でいいのかな?」「直球すぎたかな?」「柔らかい言い方がしたいんだけど…」なんてぐるぐる考えているうちに、何も言えなくなってしまうことも。そんなお悩みに応えて、この『絵でおぼえる英会話　ビジネス編』が誕生しました。

## 楽しいから続けられる!<br>充実の全27シチュエーション

本書は、職場における**27のシチュエーションを収録しています。初出勤日や自己紹介などの初歩から、同僚とのランチや退勤後の雑談、そしてメールや電話応対、会議の場**といったビジネスパーソン必須のフレーズまでさまざま。ちょっとした一言までリアルに体験できます。

これから仕事で英語を使ってみたいなと思っている人にも、今まさに仕事で英語を使っている人にもおすすめです。**まずはこの本を通じて、英語が飛び交うオフィスを体験してみてください。英語力も、そして自信も、身につくこと間違いなしです。**

# 5つの特長

## 1 Fun! 楽しい

まるでその場にいるかのよう! Real Talkingでは実際の場面を体感できるから、楽しくマンガを読むだけでフレーズがスラスラ覚えられます。主人公Annaと一緒に、さあ出かけましょう!

## 2 Useful! 役に立つ

今日から使える簡単フレーズが盛り沢山！ そのほか海外Q&Aや関連単語も併せて覚えられるから、実生活で生きてくる本当の英語力が身につきます！

## 3 Easy! 簡単

飽き性の人も心配無用！ 全てのセリフをアメリカ人ナレーターが読み上げた付属音声や、15日間完成のおすすめ学習スケジュールがついているから、手軽なのに1人でもしっかり成果が出ます！

15日間完成

Day 1 START! Day 2 Day 3 Day 4
Day 5 Day 6 Day 7 Day 8
Day 9 Day 10 Day 11 Day 12
Day 13 Day 14 Day 15 FINISH!

## 4 Only English! 本格的

本文は英語だけ！ でも心配はいりません。初めて言葉を覚える子どものように、ストーリーを楽しむうちに自然と英語を英語のまま理解できるようになります。シンプルな日常会話とはいえ、英語を英語で覚えることは真の英語力向上への最短ルートです。

## 5 Repeat! 忘れない

用途別に活用できる4種の付属音声のほか、スペリングチェックにも使えるミニテスト、ディクテーション編もついているから、何度もリピート学習できてフレーズを忘れる心配はありません。

## CONTENTS

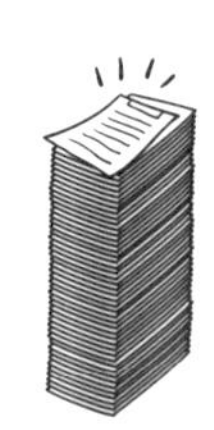

## 巻末付録

# 付属音声について

各種音声のくわしい活用方法は「おすすめ学習スケジュール&本書の使い方」（8・9ページ）をご覧ください。

## Real（リアル）

実際の英会話に近いスピードでセリフを読み上げた音声です。BGMや効果音入りなので、まるでその場にいるかのような感覚で学ぶことができます。はじめは聞き取れなくても大丈夫。わからないところは何度も聞き、だんだんと速さに慣れていきましょう。

## Shadowing（シャドーイング）

「リアル」よりもゆっくり、一語一語をはっきりと読み上げた文章です。聞き取れない部分を確認したり、リピートして発音を練習したりするのに最適です。

## Role Play（ロールプレイ）

「リアル」からAnnaのセリフのみを取り除いた音声です。Annaになりきって登場人物たちと会話してみましょう。

## Let's Review（レッツレビュー）

各スキットにおける重要フレーズの確認クイズの音声です。学習後に活用し、理解度をチェックしましょう。

## ダウンロード方法

本書の音声は「ストリーミング再生」と「音声ダウンロード」の２通りでご利用いただけます。

### ストリーミング再生

**スマホの場合**　右のQRコードを読み取り、「付属音声ダウンロード&ストリーミング再生」にアクセスしてください。

**パソコンの場合**

① 下記のURLを入力し、「付属音声ダウンロード&ストリーミング再生」にアクセスしてください。

https://bunkyosha.com/books/9784866513577/article/1

② 文響社の公式サイトにアクセスし、右上の検索バー（「書籍を検索する」と表示されている枠）に「絵でおぼえる英会話」と打ち込んでください。表示された表紙画像をクリックし、「付属音声ダウンロード&ストリーミング再生→」をクリックしてください。

https://bunkyosha.com/

### 音声ダウンロード

1 上記の①②の方法で「付属音声ダウンロード&ストリーミング再生」にアクセスしてください。

2 「絵でおぼえる英会話　ビジネス編.zip」をクリックしてください。ダウンロードが開始されます。

3 ダウンロードが完了すると、端末に「絵でおぼえる英会話　ビジネス編.zip」というファイルがダウンロードされます。解凍していただくと、中に全トラックの音声データ（MP3形式）が入っていますので、用途に合わせてご利用ください。

感動の声、
続々！

# わたしも Real Talking で 話せるようになりました！

**VOICE 01**
▶50代 山口県

**今までの英語学習は1人で黙々**と勉強している気分だったけど、**本書は会話できている感じがとても良かった**です。

**VOICE 02**
▶30代 京都府

日本語訳が書いておらず、**英語のみで自然に身につくやりかたがとても良い**と思いました。

**VOICE 03**
▶20代 滋賀県

英語のみでも、絵があるから**初心者でも読み取りやすい。**シチュエーションごとに短編ストーリーがあるので進めやすく、最後まで続けられる。

**VOICE 04**
▶30代 福岡県

**イラストや本のデザインがとにかく可愛くて**思わず手に取りました☆

※『絵でおぼえる英会話　基礎編』に寄せられた読者の皆様の声を掲載しています。

本書の投げ込みハガキ、または右のQRコードからご感想をお寄せください。

QRコードからご回答いただいたお客様には、「Dictation Book」無料PDFを配布しております。プリントアウトして繰り返しディクテーション練習するなど、学習にぜひお役立てください（アンケートの最後にアクセスリンクをご案内しています）。

15-day schedule

Real Talking

# おすすめ
# 学習スケジュール

## 15日間完成

START!

| | |
| --- | --- |
| Day 1 | 14~147ページ |
| Day 2 | 14~45ページ |
| Day 3 | 46~75ページ |
| Day 4 | 76~105ページ |
| Day 5 | 106~147ページ |
| Day 6 | 14~55ページ |
| Day 7 | 56~97ページ |
| Day 8 | 98~147ページ |
| Day 9 | 150~179ページ |
| Day 10 | 180~205ページ |
| Day 11 | 206~231ページ |
| Day 12 | 232~261ページ |
| Day 13 | 14~55ページ |
| Day 14 | 56~97ページ |
| Day 15 | 98~147ページ |

FINISH!

# 本書の使い方

## 1 想像する

まずは通しでストーリーを読んでみましょう。場面ごとに「使ってみたいフレーズ」「知らなかったフレーズ」などを頭に浮かべてみてください。

## 2 聞く

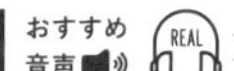

音声を聞きながら、最初は心の中で、慣れたら口に出して、セリフをまねてみましょう。1回20分程度なので、1日2回、通勤や通学などのすきま時間を活用するのがおすすめ！

## 3 話してみる

音声を聞きながら、ナレーターの抑揚や間の取り方などをまねて声に出します。慣れてきたら本を見ずに挑戦してみましょう。

## 4 書き取る

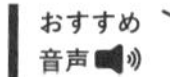

「Dictation Book」（149ページ以降）を使って、ディクテーション（ページ下部参照）の練習をしてみましょう。まずはLet's Review ①～④の空欄を使って練習をしてから「Dictation Book」に進むのがおすすめです。リスニングだけでなくスペリングも鍛えられます。

## 5 会話する

おすすめ
音声
ROLE PLAY

友人や家族と役割を分担して話してみましょう。お互いのスピーキング力向上につながります。1人の場合は、音声を活用して実際の会話のつもりで話します。自分の声を録音して、発音をチェックするのも効果的。

英語力がさらにアップ！

STEP UP

### ディクテーションとは？

「ディクテーション」とは、音声を聞いて行う書き取り練習のこと。リスニングにもスペリングの強化にも効果的です。まず音声を聞き、そのまま書き取ります。1回で全て書き取れなければ、30秒程度で区切り、繰り返し聞いて完成させます。最後までわからない部分は、その理由がリスニング（聞き取れなかった）なのか、スペリング（綴りがわからなかった）なのかを確認しましょう。同じ教材で繰り返し行うのがおすすめです。

# CHARACTERS

# キャラクター紹介

# Media ABC Company

First day of work!

REAL
01

SHADOW
-ING
32

ROLE
PLAY
59

#1

Good morning.

Good morning!
I'm Anna Kawai, a new interactive designer.

Hi, Anna.
Mr. Crary is in his office.
Thanks.

knock
knock
Come in.

Hi, Anna.
Please have a seat.

Welcome aboard.
How are you?
I'm nervous,
but excited!

You'll be fine!
Come on.
I'll show you
around the office.
Thanks.

This is your desk.
I tried to get
what you had requested.
21 inch monitor, wireless
keyboard and trackpad.

Good
morning,
Mark.

Oh, good morning.
This is Anna,
our new
interactive
designer.
This is Bob,
our front-end developer.

Hi, welcome aboard.
Hi!

This is Emily,
our senior planner.
She's an integral
part of our company.

Nice to meet you.
And you too.

This is the sales
department.
They're in a meeting now.
I'll introduce them later.
Okay.

Good morning,
Carmen.

Good morning.
Is she new?
Yeah.
Anna is
the new
designer.

Hi, Anna.
Nice to meet you.
Nice to meet you, too.
Carmen is our
administrator.

Please come and
see me after the tour.
I will.

This is the cafeteria.

Those drinks and snacks are free.

But you have to pay to use the vending machines.
I see.

Do people bring their own lunch?
Yes.

Carmen will help you with some paperwork later.
Her desk is over there.
Oh, okay.
I'll talk to her.
Thanks.

REAL
02

SHADOW
-ING
33

ROLE
PLAY
60

#2

??

Excuse me, Carmen.
Do you have a minute?
Yeah. What's up?

I want to scan this document and send it as a PDF, but I don't know how to use this machine.

Oh, okay.

In the US, letter-size paper is used often.
It's a little wider than the A4 size used in Japan.

Press the SCAN button and the machine will start.
SCAN

All done.
Great.

Thanks so much!
No problem.

REAL
03

SHADOW-ING
34

ROLE PLAY
61

#3

EMILY: Hey,
lunch buddy.
ANNA: Hey.
EMILY: Hey,
lunch buddy.
ANNA: Hey.
EMILY: Are we on for lunch
today?
ANNA: Yeah.
YUM
YUM
EMILY: Hey,
lunch buddy.
ANNA: Hey.
EMILY: Are we on for lunch
today?
ANNA: Yeah.
EMILY: What time?
ANNA: One?
EMILY: OK.
EMILY: Are we on for lunch
today?
ANNA: Yeah.
EMILY: What time?
ANNA: One?
EMILY: OK.
EMILY: Is Mike
joining us?
ANNA: I'm not sure.

EMILY: What time?
ANNA: One?
EMILY: OK.
EMILY: Is Mike joining us?
ANNA: I'm not sure.

**EMILY: Let me ask him.**
**[Emily invites Mike]**

EMILY: OK.
EMILY: Is Mike joining us?
ANNA: I'm not sure.
EMILY: Let me ask him.
[Emily invites Mike]

**EMILY: Hey.**
**MIKE: Hey.**

[Emily invites Mike]
EMILY: Hey.
MIKE: Hey.

**EMILY: Anna and I are going to lunch. Are you in?**
**MIKE: I can't take a lunch break since the deadline for this catalog is today.**

MIKE: I can't take a lunch break since the deadline for this catalog is today.

**EMILY: I see.**
**MIKE: Can we have lunch together tomorrow?**
**EMILY: Sure.**
**ANNA: Sure.**

EXPO

Hey, what do you wanna have?
Maybe a burrito?

OK. Let's go. It's 1:10 already.
My stomach is growling.

Two chicken burritos, please!
Burrito

REAL 04
SHADOW-ING 35
ROLE PLAY 62
#4

Hi, Mark.
Hi.
Hi, ladies. Back from lunch?

Yeah.
Have you had lunch?
Uh-huh.

Here you are.
Thanks.

BLAH~
BLAH

OK.
I'll talk to you later.
Okay.
Talk to you later.

Emily, can I bum a cig?
Here you are.

Anna, do you smoke too?
Oh, wait. I should have asked earlier.

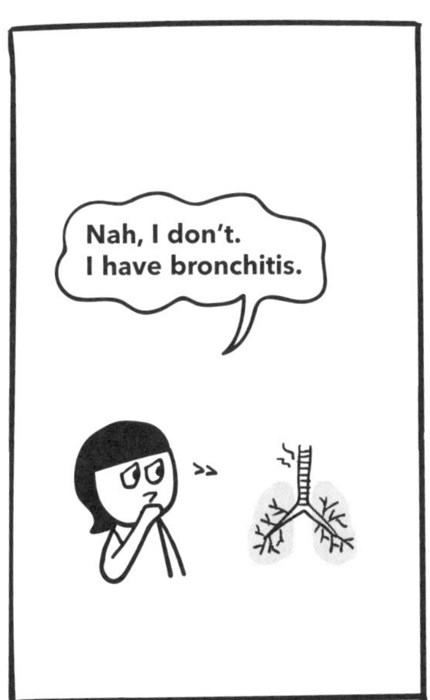
Nah, I don't.
I have bronchitis.

Oh,
I'm sorry.
You'd better
go inside.

Okay.
Talk to you
later, guys.

Anna!

Hey, Anna,
there you are.

What's up?
Mark was
just looking
for you.

Where is he?
In his office.
OK, thanks.

Oh, come in.

Achoooooo!!
Bless you.

Thanks.

You were looking for me?
Yes, I was.

I was going to ask you something,
but I just figured it out.
What was that?

I wanted to check if our banner was up.
You can check it on the admin page.

Right.
I just remembered that.
Thanks.
Sure.

REAL
06

SHADOW
-ING
37

ROLE
PLAY
64

#6

EXPO
21

Let's call it a day.

Did you finish
the image map?
Yes, I just did.
It's been a long day.

Wanna have
a quick drink?
Sounds good.

What about you,
Mike?

To take a rain check means "not now, perhaps another time".

All right.
See you
in the lobby.
A few minutes later...
Hey.
Are you
leaving
already?
Come on.
It's a quarter
to seven
already.
Haha. Yeah.
I'm about to
leave as well.
You take care.
You too.
Drive safe.

LET'S REVIEW 86
A
I'm nervous, but excited!
B
Yeah. What's up?
C
EMILY: Are we on for lunch today?
ANNA: Yeah.
EMILY: What time?
ANNA: One?
EMILY: OK.
EMILY: Is Mike joining us?
ANNA:
D

E
Maybe a burrito?
F
G
Mark was just looking for you.
Achoooooooo!!
H

**A** Welcome aboard. How are you? → p.16
**B** Excuse me, Carmen. Do you have a minute? → p.23
**C** Place them face-down. → p.24
**D** I'm not sure. → p.27
**E** Hey, what do you wanna have? → p.29
**F** Okay. Talk to you later, guys. → p.33
**G** What's up? → p.35
**H** Bless you. → p.36
**I** Let's call it a day. → p.39
**J** Yeah. I'll be right there. → p.40

REAL
07

SHADOW
-ING
38

ROLE
PLAY
65

#7

Expo
2021

Hi, Anna,
how are you doing?

Oh Matthew.

I'm doing great.
How about yourself?

I need some copies of the contract proposals from N-RUN.
Contract Proposal
by

Not just email estimates.
Mail
PDF
Contract Proposals.pdf
1.3 MB

When do you need them by?
Can I get them now?

Sorry, but I'm up to my ears in work at the moment.
I can take care of it late this afternoon.

Okay, but
I hope to get them
by five at the latest.
All right.
Thank you
in advance.

Hi, Matthew.
Here are the copies
you asked for.
Please make
sure there aren't
any pages missing.

I appreciate it.
No problem.

New Message

Send Chat Attach Address Fonts Colors Save As Draft

To: Keith@nrcompany.com

Cc:

Subject: Regarding the Logo Design

**Dear Mr. Mitchell,**

**I apologize for the delay in my reply.**
**As I have been having trouble**
**with my office email account,**
**please send all future correspondence**
**to my personal email address.**

**I would be happy to assist your**
**organization in creating**
**a logo design.**
**Mark has mentioned**
**designing your logo,**
**brochures, and newsletters.**

MEDIA ABC

Email

First, I need to confirm what kind of graphic materials you need.

After you provide me with the rough guidelines in PDF format,
I will email the drafts for you to review.

The best way to contact me
during the day is
through HelloMessage,
or by phone at 213-456-7890.

I am looking forward to
working with you.

Respectfully,
Anna Kawai

REAL
09

SHADOW
-ING
40

ROLE
PLAY
67

#9

BIP
BIP

Hello?
Hello,
may I speak to
Mr. Mitchell,
please?

May I ask
who is calling?
This is Anna Kawai
from Media ABC.

Just a moment,
please.
Okay.

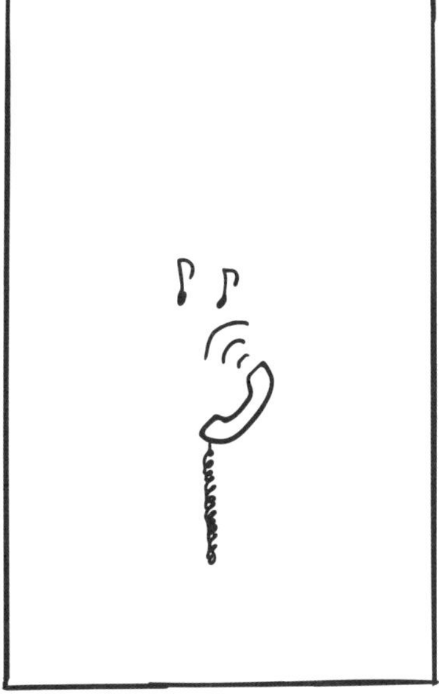

Hello, Anna.
How are you?
Fine. Thanks for asking. How about you?
Same here.

I'm calling to let you know that I just sent you an email about the logo design.

Great. I'll check it immediately.

As I mentioned in the email,
my company email account isn't working properly.

OK,
then how can I
reach you?

Please email me at
annakawai@cmail.com.
No problem,
I'll do that.

Great, thanks.
Have a nice day.
Thanks, Anna.
I'll get back
to you soon.

Email

File Edit View Go

New | X | Reply | Send/Receive Search

Mail

Inbox
Unread mail
Sent item

## Meeting today at 3 PM

[markcrary@media-abc.com]

Sent: mon/9/6/2021 1:00 PM
To: quality control@media-abc.com

**Hi, Everyone.**

**We will have a meeting today from 3 pm to 5 pm in the Conference Room.**

**Everyone in the marketing department is expected to attend.**

**The purpose of the meeting is to discuss the web marketing service that we need.**

**Thanks,**
**Mark**

Hi, Emily.
Did you get the email
about the meeting
this afternoon?
Yes, I did.

Can you
make it?
Yes,
I'll be there.

Great,
I'd like to put you
in charge of reviewing
last year's SEO.
SEO 2020
Sure,
I can do that.
SEO stands for
search engine optimization.

I think there's a related file in my folder.
SEO.txt
Good.

You'll have five to ten minutes to remind us of how we proceeded with the project last year.

Five minutes should be enough.

Probably.
That will help get everyone up to speed.
Okay.

Thanks.
I'll see you then.
See you then.

SIGH~

You need a hand?

Thanks.
You're a lifesaver!

#11

Thank you all for attending.

As you can see, there are four items to cover on the agenda.

Agenda

1. Search engine ranking
2. Improving web performance
3. Pay-per-click marketing
4. Social networking, social media marketing

First, let me start off
by saying thank you
for your outstanding
contributions to the success
of the project.

All right.

The first agenda item is
improving our search
engine ranking.
Emily,
could you briefly remind us
about last year's
successful SEO strategy?

We followed
nine essential rules
for a successful SEO strategy.

Nine essential rules for
a successful SEO strategy

1. Content is key.
2. Know your target keywords.
3. Social networks are important and highly integrated.
4. Create engaging and interesting titles.
5. Link-building drives credibility.
6. Unethical advertising will get you banned.
7. Regularly update old contents.
8. The rules literally change every day.
9. Constant feeds are necessary.

Thanks, Emily.

Let's get back to the main issue.

We've been spending a lot of money on aggressive search engine optimization.

I strongly believe
that we should cut the budget
and use
social networking websites instead.

I would like to hear your thoughts and ideas.

Yes? Mike?

REAL
12

SHADOW
-ING
43

ROLE
PLAY
70

#12

My grandmother is in critical condition in the ICU, and I'd like to see her in case anything happens.

ICU stands for intensive care unit.

Oh, I'm sorry to hear that.

How much time off do you need?

She's on the east coast, so I guess probably three to four days.

OK. You'll need to submit a request for a leave of absence.
Oh, okay.

If you need a hand, let me know.
Thanks, Mark.

Dear Frank,

I would like to request
a leave of absence due to a family matter.

My grandmother is in the ICU,
and I would like to personally
tend to her needs at this time.

I would like to request four days of leave.
I will report for work again on the 26th.

I apologize for the inconvenience.

Sincerely,
Anna Kawai

REAL
13

SHADOW
-ING
44

ROLE
PLAY
71

#13

RING
RING

Hello,
Media ABC.
This is Anna speaking.

May I speak to
Mark Clearly?
I'm sorry
but there's no one
here by that name.

Oh, I'm sorry.
I'm looking for
Mark Crary.

Oh, okay.
I'll transfer your call.
Thanks.

.....

Hello, I'm sorry but he is not at his desk at the moment.

Would you like to leave a message for him?
Yes, please.

This is Hannah Jenkins from Atman. I'd like to receive a confirmation letter in regard to the media expo.
Oh, okay.
Hannah Jenkins

Could you please ask him to call me back?
I will.
He'll be back soon.
Thanks.

Actually, I may be away from my desk for a while, so I'll call back later.
Would you like me to give you his direct extension number?
That would be great.

It's
765-432-1098.
I appreciate it.

LET'S REVIEW 87

E
F
Hi, Mark.
G
Of course.
Is everything
all right?
H

**A** By the way, can I ask you a favor? → p.47

**B** Sorry, but I'm up to my ears in work at the moment. → p.48

**C** May I ask who is calling? → p.53

**D** Can you make it? → p.57

**E** Five minutes should be enough. → p.58

**F** You need a hand? → p.59

**G** I was wondering if it would be possible to have a few days off. → p.65

**H** Hello, Media ABC. This is Anna speaking. → p.69

**I** Oh, okay. I'll transfer your call. → p.69

**J** Hello, I'm sorry but he is not at his desk at the moment. → p.70

REAL
14

SHADOW
-ING
45

ROLE
PLAY
72

#14

Hi, Anna.
Do you have a minute?
Can I see you
in my office?
Sure.

Take a seat.
Thanks.

As you know,
MG Group will be
holding a conference
next month.
9
1 2 3 4 5
6 7 8 9 10 11 12
Conference

The one we're going to participate in?
M-Vision
Gogle
MEDIA
ABC
Firenet

Right.
I'd like to hear about the progress of your project.

I began implementing the program with Emily.

How is it going?
Smoothly.
But we recently ran into some problems.

How long will it take to fix them?
We're working as fast as we can.

Good.
I know we have plenty to do, but hang in there.
Okay.

Please keep me informed of your progress.
I will.

REAL
15

SHADOW
-ING
46

ROLE
PLAY
73

#15

S-Vision
Ms.Tilla
Swanski

Hello,
S-Vision Network.

Hello,
this is Anna Kawai
from Media ABC.
May I speak
with Ms. Swanski?
I am returning her call.

Please hold
while I transfer
your call.
Thanks.

Hello,
this is Tilla speaking.
Hello, Tilla.
This is Anna
from Media ABC.

I got your message
regarding the estimate
you drew up.
Estimate
$$

Yes.
I'm sorry,
but that estimate is
for a week-long ad.
Estimate
Oh, I see.

Would you please
discard that one?
I'll send you
the revised one
immediately.

A few minutes later...

REAL
16

SHADOW-ING
47

ROLE PLAY
74

#16

Carmen Abate
all@media-abc.com
Thursday, September 26, 2021 1:27 pm
Cell Phone Usage

Inbox

Get Mail | New Message | Delete | Junk | Reply | Reply all | Forward

**From:** Carmen Abate
**To:** all@media-abc.com
**Sent:** Thursday, September 26, 2021 1:27 pm
**Subject:** Cell Phone Usage

---

Dear Everyone,

Lately, some people have been using cell phones at their desks during business hours. This is distracting to others and reduces the overall efficiency of the entire office.

Please be advised that using a cell phone during work hours could be grounds for a written warning that would be placed in your personnel file.

Thank you for your cooperation.

Carmen A. Abate

Did you read the email?

The one about using cell phones? Uh-huh.

SIGH~
The policies seem to get stricter every year.

There are surveillance cameras in the office, aren't there?
Yeah. We are being watched!

It's suffocating.

SIGH~

REAL
17
SHADOW-ING
48
ROLE PLAY
75

#17

Wedding
Invitation

Congrats, Gina!
Thanks!
Congrats!

What's going on here?

Hey, Anna!
There's something
I want to give you.

Gina & Joshua
are delighted
to invite you
to their wedding
on November 11. 2021
at three o'clock
in the afternoon.
Aquarium of the Pacific.
Long Beach, CA.
Reception to follow
RSVP to Gina & Joshua
by October 20. 2021

A wedding invitation?
Wow!
Congratulations!
You're
getting married!

Yes, I am.
Finally, huh?

I'm really happy
for you.
Thanks.
You'll come,
won't you?

When is
the big day?
It's November
11th. Please
let me know by
October 20th.

I definitely will!
I can't wait to
see you in your
wedding dress.
I'm so excited.

RSVP is French and stands for "répondez s'il vous plaît", which means "please reply."

RSVP

Please Respond By October 20. 2021

Ms. Anna Kawai

✔ Will Attend

☐ Will Not Attend

1 # of Adults (12+)

– # of Children (under 12)

Dietary Restrictions Peach allergy

(Please list any dietary restrictions.)

REAL
18
SHADOW
-ING
49
ROLE
PLAY
76

#18

Hey, Anna. We're going
to the Lazy Dog
for happy hour.
Can you make it at 6:20?

I'm sorry,
but can I take
a rain check?
I have something
to do this evening.

That's too bad.
We'll probably
be there until 8.
Can you just swing
by before then?

I don't think
I can make it today.
Sorry.

Loser.
What did you just say?

I said loser!
You're such a party pooper.

Calm down, Anna. You know he's a jerk.
Don't even answer him. You'd better talk to Mark about this.
Okay.

Dear Mark,

I would like to report an incident
that happened in the office yesterday, October 23rd,
and to ask for your advice in this matter.

My coworker Dean referred to me as a "loser"
and treated me in a very disrespectful way.
This was not an isolated incident.
I have been the victim of his harassment
on several occasions.

I would like to speak to you in person
about how to handle this situation
and to hear your advice
about the appropriate course of action.

Thank you,
Anna Kawai

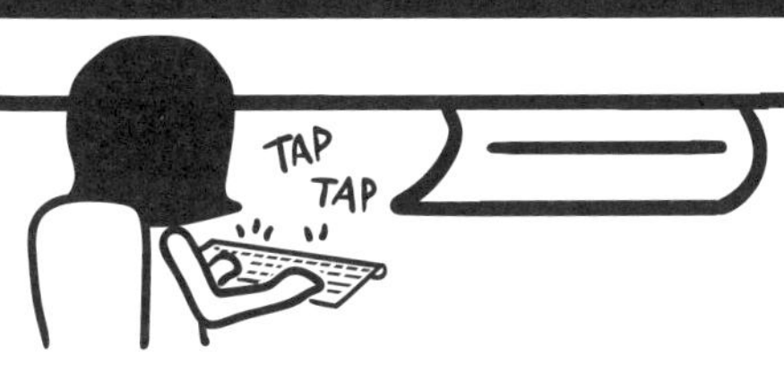

The next day...
Morning, Anna.
Do you have a minute?
Sure.
Can I see you
in my office?
Okay.

I just got your email and wanted to hear exactly what happened yesterday.

LOSER !!
BLAH
BLAH~ BLAH~

I see.
If you want,
I can report it and
HR will handle it.
That would be great.

Okay.
That seems
the best thing to do
based on
his usual behavior.
Thanks for understanding.

REAL
19

SHADOW
-ING
50

ROLE
PLAY
77

#19

I have a horrible migraine.
I'd better call in sick today.

Mark

Hello. This is Mark. I'm not available at the moment. Please leave a message and I'll get back to you as soon as I can.

Hi, Mark. This is Anna.

If there is any problem, please give me a call. I'll talk to you later.

A few minutes later...

Over-the-counter medicine
can be bought without
a medical prescription.

**Thanks.**
**See you tomorrow.**

**Hope you**
**feel better soon**
**and I'll see you tomorrow.**

LET'S REVIEW 88

E
F
G
Thanks.
You'll come,
won't you?
H
Sorry.

**You should take some over-the-counter medicine.**

Over-the-counter medicine can be bought without a medical prescription.

**A** Take a seat. → p.77

**B** We're working as fast as we can. → p.79

**C** May I speak with Ms. Swanski?
I am returning her call. → p.81

**D** I will get in touch with you after reviewing it. → p.83

**E** It's suffocating. → p.87

**F** What's going on here? → p.89

**G** I'm really happy for you. → p.90

**H** I don't think I can make it today. → p.93

**I** I'd better call in sick today. → p.99

**J** I've had a horrible migraine since
I woke up and it's not letting up. → p.101

REAL
20

SHADOW
-ING
51

ROLE
PLAY
78

#20

"cc" stands for "carbon copy" and means to send a copy of an email or document to someone other than the primary addressee.

Sounds great.
We seem to be a week ahead of schedule.
!!

Really?
I will probably arrange the call for Monday.

Oh, one more thing.
We have a board meeting early next month. I'd like to present our new look there.
Can you finish it before then?
MEDIA ABC

It's almost done.
Great.

When can I expect to get the final design?
PDF
final-design.pdf

Just give me a few more days.
11

I'll have it to you by the 13th.
Perfect. Thanks for your hard work.

TAP
TAP

REAL
21
SHADOW
-ING
52
ROLE
PLAY
79

#21

MEDIA ABC

Flower delivery
for Ms. Anna Kawai.
She's in the marketing
department.
Go straight down
the hall.
Thanks!
Is that for Anna?
Wow.
She's in the
corner office.

Ms. Anna Kawai?
Yes?

Flower delivery for you.

Me?
From whom?
There's a note in the basket.
You have a wonderful day.

wow~

Hey lady,
who sent
the flowers?
No idea.
I'm about to
check the card.

What does it say?
"Happy
birthday".

Happy birthday, Anna!!
We wanted to
surprise you!
They're from all of us!

Thank you so much!
You made my day!

REAL
22

SHADOW
-ING
53

ROLE
PLAY
80

#22

Cheese
Chips
Pretzels

Hey.
Is that....
Ugh...
I forgot
the name of it!

What is it called?
It's on the tip of my
tongue.

Uh,
ePad mini?
That's
right.

Do you mind me asking
where you bought it?
I got it
online.

I'm not sure which store it was though.

??

How much did it cost?

It was listed at $699,
but I had a promotion code from the manufacturer and was luckily able to save about $100.

Amazing! Thanks.

I'm actually looking for a touch pad tablet. How do you like it?
??

In terms of portability,
it's perfect.
But,
the screen seems
a little dull to me.
I see.

I may go out shopping
to compare
some firsthand.

Good luck.

Thanks.
You're welcome.

REAL 23
SHADOW-ING 54
ROLE PLAY 81

#23

HEY~!!

Hi, Anna!
How have you been?
Good.
How about you?
I've been
very busy lately.
We haven't run into
each other in ages,
even though we work
in the same building.
You're right.
So, how's work?
Sometimes
it's very challenging.
But I do enjoy working
with my colleagues.

Emily says that you're a good team player.
I'm glad to hear that.
By the way, have you noticed any recent changes in your office?
What do you mean?
Well, you know how this business market is getting smaller and worse, and many companies have begun reorganizing their departments?

Uh-huh.
The economy is in bad shape.

A few employees in my company were laid off in the last three months.
Oh, no.... That's too bad.

Has anyone been let go in your office?
Um...
Not that I know of.

SIGH~

REAL
24

SHADOW
-ING
55

ROLE
PLAY
82

#24

!!....

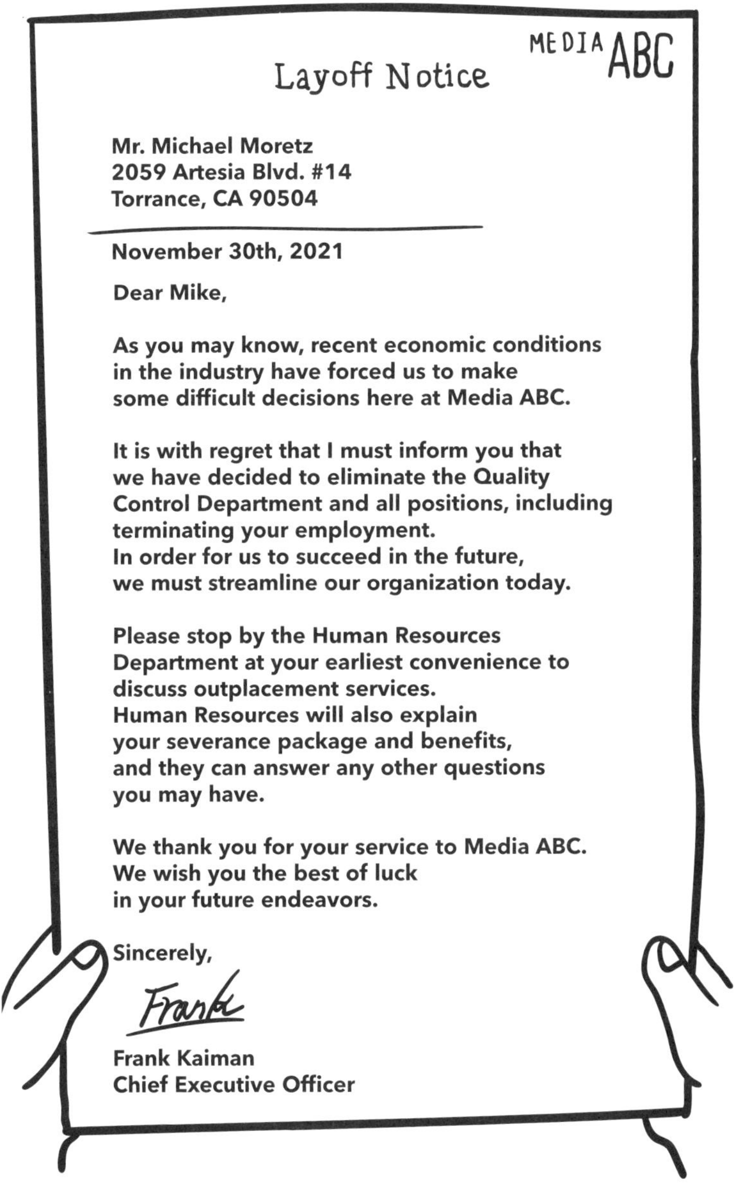

MEDIA ABC

# Layoff Notice

Mr. Michael Moretz
2059 Artesia Blvd. #14
Torrance, CA 90504

November 30th, 2021

Dear Mike,

As you may know, recent economic conditions in the industry have forced us to make some difficult decisions here at Media ABC.

It is with regret that I must inform you that we have decided to eliminate the Quality Control Department and all positions, including terminating your employment.
In order for us to succeed in the future, we must streamline our organization today.

Please stop by the Human Resources Department at your earliest convenience to discuss outplacement services.
Human Resources will also explain your severance package and benefits, and they can answer any other questions you may have.

We thank you for your service to Media ABC.
We wish you the best of luck in your future endeavors.

Sincerely,

Frank

Frank Kaiman
Chief Executive Officer

. . . .

I'm so sorry Mike.
I just heard the news. I don't know what to say.

I'm okay guys.
Heard Jake is leaving too.

He already left an hour ago.
Yeah? I didn't know that.

Let's keep in touch, okay?
Call me this weekend. We'll have a drink.
Definitely.

REAL
25
SHADOW
-ING
56
ROLE
PLAY
83

#25

$$
ROUTE
66
ROAD
TRIPS

Your paycheck, Anna.
Thanks.

Hmm.....

Hey,
Did you get paid for working overtime?
Huh?

The overtime hours we worked last month. Wasn't it about four hours?
Yeah, it was.

But we won't be able to get paid for that.
Why not?

If we work on salary, usually we won't get paid working for overtime.
Salary
$$$$$$$$/1year
Hourly
$/1hour
Oh...

I was just curious because I heard Gina gets overtime pay.

It's because she works hourly.
I see.

# How to Deposit a Paycheck at an ATM

**1.** Detach the check from the pay stub.

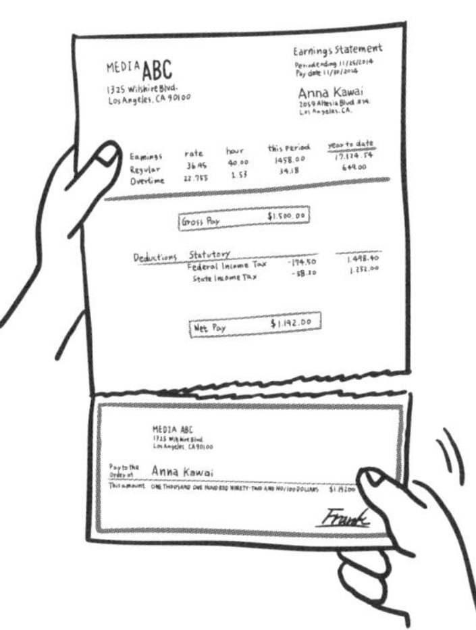


**2.** Write your signature on the back.

**3.** Insert your ATM card, then follow the instructions and insert the check into the machine.

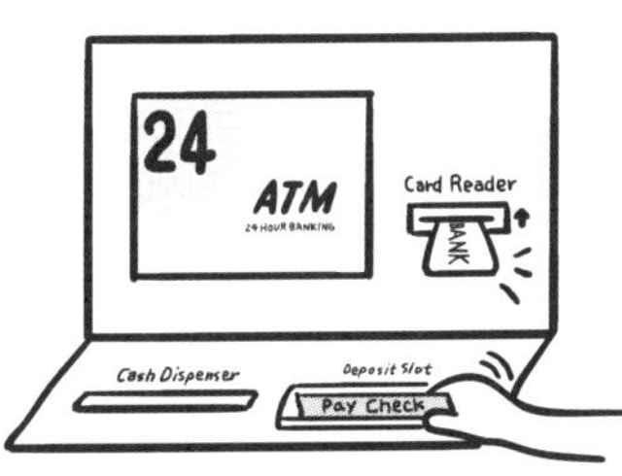

Good afternoon.
Thank you for taking time out of your day to be with us.

I'm pleased to introduce Mr. Steve Morrison.

Mr. Morrison is the Senior Project Manager for Accessibility at Firenet.

He is in charge of Accessibility across the product line.

Let's welcome Mr. Steve Morrison with a warm round of applause.

Hello, everyone.
Thank you.
I'm glad to be here
with you today.
Before I begin,
I'd like to learn a little bit
about your experience.
Are there any
software platform
developers in the group?
CLAP CLAP CLAP CLAP
CLAP

REAL
27
SHADOW-ING
58
ROLE PLAY
85

#27

BLAH~
BLAH~
BLAH~
HA HA
HAHA!
Ms.Chen!!
Mark!!

Ms. Chen.
I'd like you to meet
Ms. Anna Kawai.

She's one of
our most talented
designers.

Anna,
this is Ms. Rachel Chen.
OH!

She is
my former supervisor
and is currently
a vice president
at WJ Company.

Hi, Anna.

It's great to finally meet you.

I've heard a lot about your outstanding work from Mark.

I'm so flattered to hear that, Ms. Chen.

I've read your book about social media marketing.

It was really inspiring.

By the way, congratulations on the successful launch of the new website.
You did a good job.
Thank you.

But it wasn't just me, it was my team, including Anna.

To Media ABC!
Cheers!

A
To: Mark
Cc: Frank
Subject: Ad Completed
"cc" stands for "carbon copy" and means to send a copy of an email or document to someone other than the primary addressee.

Sounds great.
B

C
"Happy birthday".

D

E
F
Good.
How about you?
Has anyone been
let go in your office?
Um...
G
Hey,
H
Huh?

**A** I sent it to you and cc'd Frank this morning. → p.107
**B** We seem to be a week ahead of schedule. → p.108
**C** What does it say? → p.113
**D** Thank you so much! You made my day! → p.113
**E** What is it called? It's on the tip of my tongue. → p.115
**F** Hi, Anna! How have you been? → p.119
**G** Not that I know of. → p.121
**H** Did you get paid for working overtime? → p.127
**I** I'd like you to meet Ms. Anna Kawai. → p.133
**J** We've referred to your book in a team meeting. → p.134

MEDIA ABC

OH!

REAL
28

How do I get a job?

## 1. Job Opening

# INTERACTIVE DESIGNER

DEPARTMENT: Marketing, Design, Web

CITY: Los Angeles, CA    TYPE: Full-Time

- Description: Media ABC is looking for a designer to join its Digital Media Group.
- Education background: Bachelor's degree in a creative discipline
- Work experience: Two to five years in a related field
- Salary: $30k-60k/year
- Benefits: Medical / Dental / Vision Insurance / Pension
- Free coffee & drinks

"k" is short for "kilo," which means "thousand."

## 2. Submitting a Cover Letter

# Anna Kawai

2059 Altesia Blvd. #14, Los Angeles, CA
(213) 456-7890 * annakawai@cmail.com

---

December 15, 2020
Media ABC, Inc.
1325 Wilshire Blvd.
Los Angeles, CA 90100

Dear Recruiting Manager:

Attached is my resume in response to
your ad on JOB.com.

I understand your that company is currently seeking
an experienced designer to assist in the further growth of
your company, and I would like to be considered
for the position.

I have a Bachelor of Arts degree in multimedia
and three years of relevant work experience.
In addition, I am self-motivated, have
strong organizational skills, exacting attention to detail,
and the ability to work with a diverse range of people.
I am confident that I would be a strong asset to
your company.

I welcome the opportunity to discuss my qualifications
with you and to learn more about your company, and the
available position.
Please contact me at at (213)456-7890 or via email at
annakawai@cmail.com.

Sincerely,
Anna Kawai
Enclosed: Resume

3. Submitting a Resume

# Anna Kawai

2059 Altesia Blvd. #14, Los Angeles, CA (213)456-7890 *annakawai@cmail.com

## OBJECTIVE

**Seeking a position as a multimedia designer in a team-oriented environment.**

## EDUCATION

**Newrun College, Tokyo, Japan**
**BA in multimedia, 2017**
**Honors Program, 3.68 GPA**

## EXPERIENCE

**ThinkBig, Inc. Tokyo, Japan**
**Interactive Designer, 2019-20**

**Newrun College, Tokyo, Japan**
**Digital Production Lab Manager, 2017-19**

## SKILLS

**IT Skills: Action Script, CSS, XHTML, JavaScript**
**Applications: Adobe Photoshop, Adobe Illustrator, Adobe InDesign, Apple DVD Studio Pro**

# 4. Arranging an Interview

Hello.

Hello.
May I talk to Ms. Anna Kawai?

This is she.

This is Mark Crary,
a marketing director
at Media ABC.

Oh!

Hello,
Mr. Crary.

I'm calling you
to arrange an interview
sometime this week.
How is Thursday?

Thursday
sounds good
to me.

Great.
What about two
in the afternoon?

Okay.
I'll be there at two.

Is there anything
I need to bring?

Bring
your printed
portfolio, please.

All right.
I will see you then.

## 5. First Job Interview

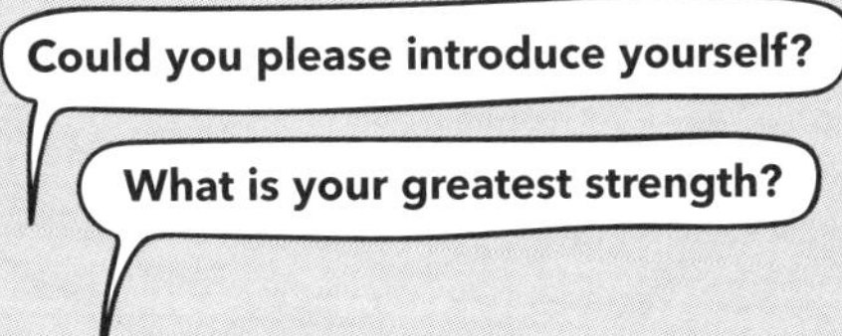

## 6. Sending a Thank-you email

New Message

Send

Account▾

To: markcrary@media-abc.com

Subject: Thank you for the interview

Dear Mr. Crary,

Thank you for the opportunity to meet with you today
and to interview for the position of interactive designer.
I learned a great deal about Media ABC,
and am confident that my skills and abilities are
a perfect match for the position.

I sincerely appreciate your time today,
and look forward to hearing back from you about
joining your company.

Thank you for your consideration.

Sincerely,
Anna Kawai

Anna Kawai
(213) 456-7890 * annakawai@cmail.com

Fingers crossed!

SEND!!

7. Second Job Interview

8. Congratulations!

# Dictation Book

ディクテーション編

CHARACTERS

# キャラクター紹介

# Media ABC Company

SHADOW
-ING
32

knock
knock

Cheese
Chips

SHADOW
-ING
33

#2

SCAN

SHADOW
-ING
34

#3

EMILY:

ANNA:

EMILY:

ANNA:

YUM YUM

EMILY:
ANNA:
EMILY:

EMILY:

ANNA:

EMILY:
EMILY:
MIKE:
EMILY:
MIKE:
EMILY:
MIKE:
EMILY:
ANNA:

EXPO

Burrito

#4

BLAH~
BLAH

Anna!

Achoooooo!!

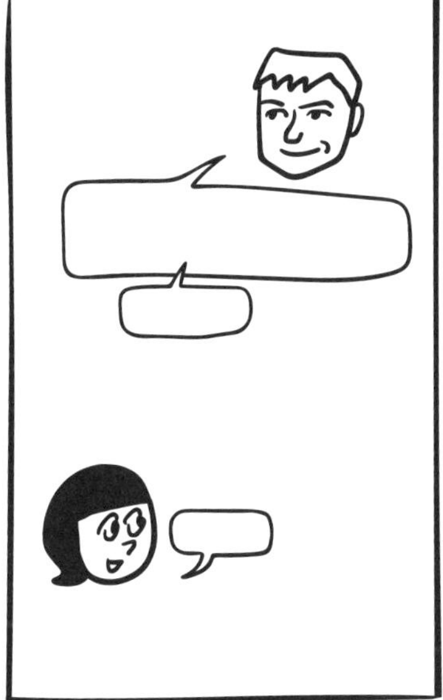

SHADOW
-ING
37

#6

EXPO
21
5

A few minutes later...

SHADOW
-ING
38

#7

Expo
2021

Expo 2021

Contract Proposal
by

Mail
X
PDF
Contract Proposals.pdf
1.3 MB

New Message

Send Chat Attach Address Fonts Colors Save As Draft

To: keith@nrcompany.com

Cc:

Subject: Regarding the Logo Design

MEDIA ABC

November Conference

Email
PDF
November
Conference

SHADOW
-ING
40

#9

BIP
BIP

sorry,

Email

File Edit View Go

New | X | Reply | Send/Receive Search

Mail

Inbox
Unread mail
Sent item

Meeting today at 3 PM

[markcrary@media-abc.com]

Sent: mon/9/6/2021 1:00 PM
To: quality control@media-abc.com

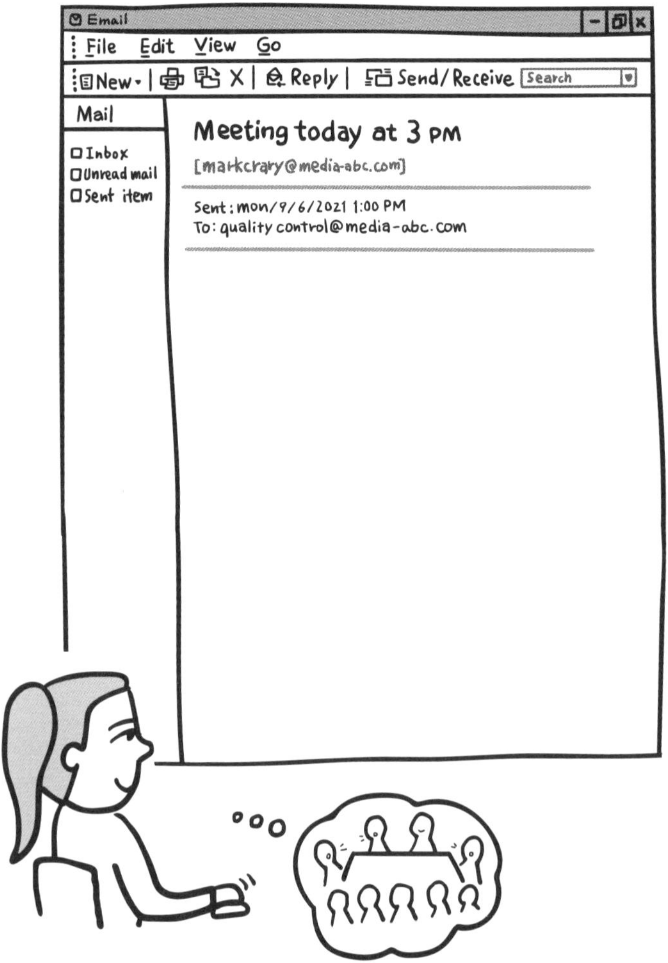

SEO 2020

SEO.txt
SEO
in 2020,

SIGH~

#11

Agenda

1. Search engine ranking
2. Improving web performance
3. Pay-per-click marketing
4. Social networking,
social media marketing

# Nine essential rules for a successful SEO strategy

1. Content is key.
2. Know your target keywords.
3. Social networks are important and highly integrated.
4. Create engaging and interesting titles.
5. Link-building drives credibility.
6. Unethical advertising will get you banned.
7. Regularly update old contents.
8. The rules literally change every day.
9. Constant feeds are necessary.

I think
we have to try..

SHADOW
-ING
43

#12

TAP TAP

SHADOW
-ING
44

#13

RING
RING

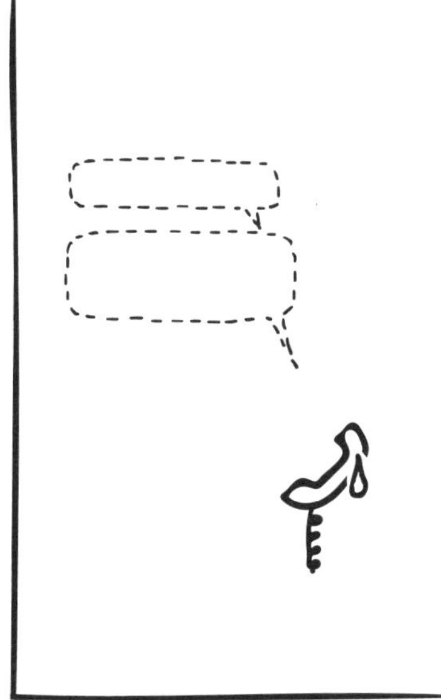

.....
Hannah
Jenkins

SHADOW
-ING
45

#14

9
1 2 3 4 5
6 7 8 9 10 11 12
Conference

M-Vision
Gogle
MEDIA
ABC
Firenet

SHADOW
-ING
46

#15

S-Vision
Ms.Tilla
Swanski

Estimate
$$
Detail
$900
$859
$1200
$1510
Estimate
X!!
Estimate
X!!

A few minutes later...
DING

SHADOW
-ING
47

#16

Inbox
Carmen Abate
all@media-abc.com
Thursday, September 26, 2021 1:27 pm
Cell Phone Usage

From: Carmen Abate
To: all@media-abc.com
Sent: Thursday, September 26, 2021 1:27 pm
Subject: Cell Phone Usage

SIGH~
SIGH~

SHADOW
-ING
48

#17

Wedding
Invitation

Gina & Joshua
are delighted
to invite you
to their wedding
on November 11. 2021
at three o'clock
in the afternoon.
Aquarium of the Pacific.
Long Beach, CA.
Reception to follow
RSVP to Gina & Joshua
by October 20. 2021

RSVP

Please Respond By October 20, 2021

Ms. Anna Kawai

✓ Will Attend

☐ Will Not Attend

1 # of Adults (12+)

– # of Children (under 12)

Dietary Restrictions Peach allergy

(Please list any dietary restrictions.)

SHADOW
-ING
49

#18

LOSER !!
TAP
TAP

The next day...

LOSER !!
BLAH
BLAH~BLAH~

SHADOW
-ING
50

#19

Mark

A few minutes later...

SHADOW
-ING
51

#20

MEDIA ABC

To: Mark
Cc: Frank
Subject: Ad Completed

MEDIA ABC

PDF
final-design.pdf
11
TAP
TAP

SHADOW
-ING
52

#21

MEDIA ABC

Thanks!

WOW~

SHADOW
-ING
53

#22

Cheese
Chips

SHADOW-ING
54

#23

HEY~!!

SIGH~

SHADOW
-ING
55

#24

!!....

MEDIA ABC

# Layoff Notice

**Mr. Michael Moretz**
**2059 Artesia Blvd. #14**
**Torrance, CA 90504**

**November 30th, 2021**

Frank

SHADOW
-ING
56

#25

$$
ROUTE
66
ROAD
TRIPS

Salary
$$$$$$$$/1 year
Hourly
$/1 hour

# How to Deposit a Paycheck at an ATM

1.

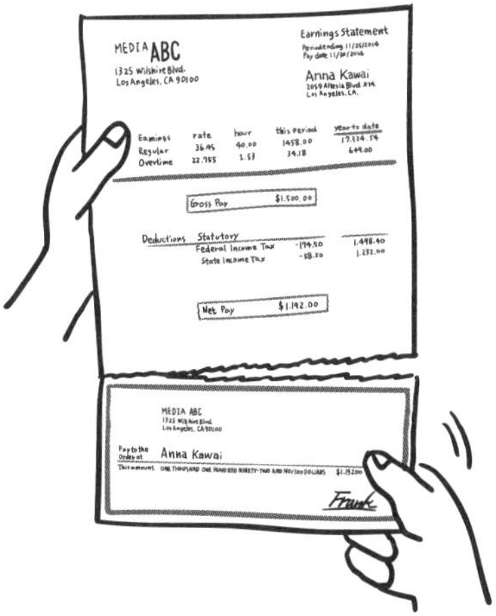

2.

3.

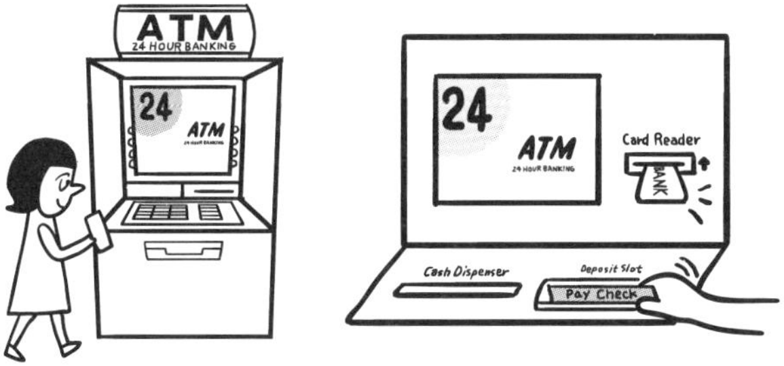

#26

CLAP
CLAP
CLAP
CLAP

Website Design
Seminar

CLAP CLAP CLAP CLAP
CLAP

SHADOW-ING
58

#27

BLAH~
BLAH~
BLAH~
HA HA
HAHA!
Ms.Chen!!
Mark!!

OH!

Now, SNS!

HAHA

著者

**エリー・オー**

Ellie Oh

アメリカの現地シニアデザイナー、フィリピンの国際学校ディレクター、韓国の英語講師および著者として多様な経歴をもつ。日常のさまざまなシーンに即したリアルな英語と異文化理解に関心が深い。幼稚園児から社会人、シニアに至るまで、幅広い年齢層の生徒に教えた経験をもとに「生きた英語」を伝えるための活動を行っている。自身がアメリカの企業に勤めたときの苦労や発見をもとに、本書を執筆した。

# 絵でおぼえる英会話　ビジネス編

2021年4月13日　第1刷発行

| | |
|---|---|
| 著　者 | エリー・オー |
| 編　者 | ターシャ・キム／アンナ・ヤン |
| デザイン | 小寺練 |
| イラスト | サンダースタジオ |
| 翻訳協力 | 三嶋圭子 |
| 校　正 | 株式会社ぷれす |
| DTP制作 | 五木田裕之 |
| 英文校閲 | リサ・ウィルカット／原田麗衣 |
| 音声録音・編集 | ELEC（一般財団法人 英語教育協議会） |
| 編　集 | 平沢拓＋一柳沙織 |
| 発行人 | 山本周嗣 |
| 発行所 | 株式会社文響社<br>〒105-0001<br>東京都港区虎ノ門2-2-5　共同通信会館9F<br>ホームページ　https://bunkyosha.com<br>お問い合わせ　info@bunkyosha.com |
| 印刷・製本 | 中央精版印刷株式会社 |

ISBN978-4-86651-357-7　Printed in Japan